Don't Turn The Projector Off!

Matt LaFreniere

Unsolicited Press Books are distributed to the trade by
Ingram.
Printed in the United States of America.
ISBN: 978-1-947021-39-6

Many thanks to the editors of the following journals, who
first published versions of these poems: *Diverse Voices
Quarterly, Dunes Review, Jet Fuel Review, Main Street Rag,
Pilgrimage Magazine, Rat's Ass Review, Schuylkill Valley
Journal, Spry Literary Magazine, Wild Violet.*

Contents

Fade In

"Don't turn the projector off! No! No! It gets black and we disappear!"

— *Jason, The Purple Rose of Cairo (1985)*

You know it, on 2nd Street,
3rd Street, any street near you,
on Elm, Main, Hennessy,
you know it.

The red carpet bubbles, folds over
and churns while popcorn spews.
We're stippled clay under its seal
warped by flimsy slopes; we're choked
light from sunless surface,

you know,
combusting reflections.

I.

Matt Thinks of a Dream Sequence

"Give them pleasure. The same pleasure they have when they
wake up from a nightmare."
                                              — Alfred Hitchcock

When I look back on her, that tiger
in dreams, my childhood ancient
my sage, claw pointing like a wrinkled

finger, there is, like everything, only
imagination, all that there ever was then.
My father said she came from a centipede's

bite, born from my slumberous roll
over pincers — from Hell's coarse-
haired womb, its nighttime miracles

of legs and slithers and solitude.
She was a tiger of the night,
I'd ride her through my days;

she was my guide, my sojourner,
my ferryman. She stepped
on bones, crossed black sands,

climbed through jungles to dark
peaks — and we look across my land:
My mother endlessly drapes

lights around a needleless tree;
my father walks his dog into
forever; Phil, sprawled

on the lawn, considers the birds;
Joyce rolls ankles with each
high-heeled step; Esme closes

herself with her journal's lid
like a manhole cover; and Rose and Jack,
so sweet, crawl in their sheets like centipedes.

The Veld

"All the animals here are like that. They have to be in order to survive."
      — John Patterson, *The Ghost and the Darkness* (1996)

Esme says my poems are boring.
Every word is too much, she says,
use words that make you sound like you're

an actual person. My students think
my poems are great, clever and dark
in all the right ways. Does she know she births

her love for me like poems? She prowls with it
through her imagination's veld (*see, what
the hell is a veld?*), she lopes to a tree

for delivery, she pushes it out in heat
and strain, licks it clean, eats the sack of blood
and womb-life. She's satisfied in its blind wonder.

She licks again when she doesn't have to
as it rolls for the first time in the dirt.

Birthdays

"You…are…my…lucky…star…"

— Ellen Ripley, *Alien* (1979)

When Rose was born she looked
bewildered, as one does, I guess.
The doctor cupped her head with his palm
like an oracle; her eyes flinched like a liar's.

I thought she'd look as Fitzgerald's
Dutch sailors looked: on a fresh, green
breast of the new world. The room's light
sharpened, the machines buzzed, the haste

deepened. I thought of *Alien*, how
Ridley Scott rendered birth — all pulsation
and blood and panic. When I was born
my mother bled; I looked at the world and hissed.

Before they stitched her up I scurried
to the cold and the steel and the fluorescence.

Intentions

"Our little girl learned about life and death the other day."
— Bill, *Kill Bill Vol. 2* (2004)

Rose saw him first;
he must've skulked under
the cabinet's abutment, then through

the crack between the dishwasher
and its cave carved out in the island.
Mouse hole, she announced

in her two-year-old amazement,
when back in the living room,
an accusatory finger pointing

to the kitchen's silence. *Mouse hole*,
she'd say, pointing to nothing in particular,
in her crib at 3 am, in her car seat

at the woman on the corner
of Roland and 36th. I set traps
with cheese and peanut butter

and tofu, but he slipped them.
I bought glue traps — after all,
I respected his resolve, his stealth.

Dat's mouse, Rose said,
one morning when I forgot

to check the trap before she wandered

into the kitchen. I googled his safe
removal, how to unstick his snout,
his little paws. Cooking oil,

a blog suggested. I put the trap
in a cardboard box, lifted it 40 degrees,
poured around his sides, a dabble

an inch in front of his glue-caked whiskers.
Rose watched as the oil hit his lips.
He choked twice, then stopped moving.

All Shook Up

"I gotta hand it to you…you were cooler than cool."
— Elvis, *True Romance* (1993)

Almost like a dance, like an Elvis
impersonation, inward knees to outward
and all that. Esme wanted something
across the room, a water cup, maybe,

not something necessary, but something
reached for out of muscle memory.
I had just wheeled Jack to the nursery
like a newly discovered serum,
nurses abreast serious and concentrated.

When I got back there she was,
all shook up, a zombie Elvis dancing
on joints strained from life-giving.

But, her knees couldn't un-know the dance
like her spine could never know the dance.

Uprising

"…but they'll never take our freedom!"
— William Wallace, *Braveheart* (1995)

Braveheart is on.
Esme and the kids sleep upstairs
above Mel Gibson's battle cries.

It's the faux band of brothers speech,
the one where Wallace
rallies his Scotsmen for the first time

against Longshanks' impossible army —
the speech about dying in your bed
thinking of the only chance you had to fight
if you did indeed not fight.

I'm alone in the dark.
I mistake the TV's flicker
for movement on the rug —
a neurotic uprising:

how can I retreat to my family
with all this seeming mobilization,
the ants and roaches and mice?

By now their lords have called them,
they've gathered out of obligation

armed with fallen spaghetti strands,

sharpened bits of rice, drywall shields
and shards of stripped-screw slag.

The exterminator will be here in a fortnight

and the army feels the moment on whiskers,
on coarse hairs, on translucent wings
beating anxiously.

I thought I heard an awful scurry,
the small scratching of kitchen tile.

I thought I heard a mouse emerge,
give a fine speech.
I thought I heard a roach
elbow the roach beside him,
hiss something like: *What the hell
did that rodent say?*

I thought I heard a charge
like a thousand wings fluttering,
like the evolution of claws,

the soft clank of the radiator,
the slow pillage of bedsheets.

Things I Can Never Tell Jack

"But for Timothy Treadwell, this bear was a friend, a savior."
— Werner Herzog, *Grizzly Man (2005)*

Jack can sit now, and he loves the world
curiously, hungrily, like a little bear,
clumsy and unforgiving, holding on to me
to balance with impossible submission.
There's a great moment in *Grizzly Man* —
Werner Herzog's strange documentary —
When Treadwell, the subject, ever the poet,
hovers over a bear's big, berry-filled
ball of shit. *This was just inside of her,*
he says. *It was in her.* He pats the mound
with his cupped palm. Behind his voice,
the stream toddles, the wind gurgles
the camera's microphone, and we understand
the heartbreak of doubt. There are things
I can never tell Jack that he'll always know,
one way or another, imprints like heat —
downed alders in a forged path, a rock pawed
then tweaked in a stream. In the end,
a bear ate Treadwell, and who knows
how Treadwell actually submitted to death.
Jack chews a knuckle of the fist I've made
around his hand; he looks at me like he
understands I'm thinking of captivity,
he chews my knuckle like he understands
my captivity.

Hey Daddy

"Do you share my madness?"
— Viktor Frankenstein, *Mary Shelley's Frankenstein* (1994)

Hey Daddy, how did dino-saws got extinct?
Oh. Am I free years old?
Oh. Are we driving realwy fast?

Her questions like wind through grass,
like a current's reach before the thunder.

Hey Daddy, dhere's a monstah ovah dhere.
Not a monster, Rose, that's just a street painting,

I say as I'm thinking of *Frankenstein* —
not Shelley's, but Deniro's silly rendition.

But was it a monstah?
Naw, Rosie. Monsters only exist in books and movies.
I dun wanna monstah in my movie, okay?

She meets my eyes in the rearview.
She's trying to fit the pieces together.

II.

Partial Custody

"Magic is the bloodstream of the universe. Forget all you know, or think you know."
                                    — High Aldwin, *Willow* (1988)

Forget all you know, or think you know...
I remembered that line from the trailer,
same with: *Magic is the bloodstream of the universe.*

After the movie, Joyce rubbed dad's head
while he drove; we were cloaked in fall's grey-dark —
forget all you know or think you know.

Black and white cookies before back to Mom's,
I felt chosen sitting on top of the store's picnic table
(Magic is the bloodstream of the universe).

We drove back to Mom's in silence,
Dad jerked his head from Joyce's hand.
Forget all you know or think you know.

Mom met me at the door. *We saw* Willow!
I squealed (I must've assumed she'd know
that magic is the bloodstream of the universe).

Dad eased out of the driveway; I heard
his Buick chunk and sputter and spit.
Magic is the bloodstream of the universe.
Forget all you know or think you know.

We'd All Be Clean

My sister Emily would pound her pillow
with her face each night before sleep; she'd moan,
rhythmic as the water's slap of a boat's hull,
eerie as the Divine Liturgy.

We asked her why, what possessed her to do
such a thing. *It helps me sleep,* her only
answer. I'd listen through the wall,
stare through the dark at the ceiling

like I stared at candles in pre-Mass moments.
There was no contemplation, no self-
examination, just fear — cold and petulant.
I was thinking of what skulked inside her,

what strange entity entered her backyard's
consciousness, what rogue rummaged through
her trashcans, what patio-covered filth
she would've cleaned up each morning.

If I could have helped her I would have.
I would have pinned her down with gags
of vestments, doused her body in droves
of tap water, whispered: *The power of Christ compels you.*

The moon would pour over leafless branches.
The night's critters would rustle through the grass.
Something would scurry across the patio.
In the morning it would be clean. We'd all be clean.

Burning

"Smelled like...victory."
— Major Kilgore, *Apocalypse Now* (1979)

I burned GI Joes with my buddy Jake.
We were ten; it was the end of summer.
They were plastic, the flame wouldn't always take:
I'd hold the lighter hard, singe my thumb, fake

manliness, squash the pain. I remember,
when burning Joes with my buddy Jake,
my uncle OD'd on his couch; he looked awake,
Mom said, war in his belly like embers.

They were plastic, the flame wouldn't always take,
you'd have to be thorough, you'd have to wait
out the tedium in each plastic member.
We burned GI Joes, me and Jake,

after the silence of my uncle's wake
which took something like forever.
They were plastic, the flame wouldn't always take.
We grew impatient; we'd simulate

our best napalm efforts — gas and fire.
I burned GI Joes with my buddy Jake;
they were plastic, the flame wouldn't always take.

Far-Off Storms

"All work and no play…"
— Jack Torrance, *The Shining* (1980)

I know I won't be able to sleep much.
We watched *The Shining*, and now
Joyce talks of hurricanes, earthquakes.
Tomorrow we'll go to the beach,
Joyce'll talk of hurricanes, earthquakes.
I know I won't be able to sleep much.
Tomorrow we'll go to the beach;
we'll pick sand out of ham Italians,
and I know I won't be able to sleep much.
I'll bury horseflies then unbury them,
Dad'll pick sand out of his Italian, joke:
All work and no play makes Matt a dull boy,
and I know I won't be able to sleep much.
The surf will surge from far-off storms,
I'll bury horseflies then unbury them.
All work and no play makes Matt a dull boy.
I'll tell him to quit it, it's not funny.
The surf will surge from far-off storms,
I know I won't be able to sleep much.
Joyce'll walk me to the water; Dad'll want a picture.
I know I won't be able to sleep much.
Smile like 'ol Jack Nicholson, he'll Joke.
I'll tell him to quit it, it's not funny.
After the picture Joyce'll hug me hard
and I know.

Galaxies

"...help me take this mask off."
— Darth Vader, *Return of the Jedi* (1983)

Every time I watch *Return of the Jedi*
becomes every time I watched *Return of the Jedi*
with Grandpa. Dad would drop me off,
hit light speed heading to town.
Grandpa nodded, with Obi-Wan's wisdom,
to his VCR, and he gathered me under his arm
like a sickly emperor. I liked the Ewoks,
the brilliant lights of the film.
I liked when the plot paused for a father
to love his son: ships of the alliance
suspended in space, the empire's crumble
staunched for Luke to lift Vader's mask.
But that's not our story. There are no
brilliant lights. Grandpa would fall
asleep in the opening credits, and wake
to dad materializing in the driveway
to collect me. Dad would wait in the car
for me to saunter out of the house. Grandpa
watched from the window, a galaxy far away.

To Grandmothers

She blinked like mid-June nightfall
and the world pruned, wobbled away like spilled
from a raisin box. She blinked like street and sky
met in her eyelids' crease, where beetles hum

in reeds and lazy street lights clack.
She blinked as if she whisked the rippled sky
orange, with her fingers, down her tired road
to sun's impatient embers. The same blink

each time she handed my mother, from boxes
at her feet, a chipped figurine, a glass-globed
grasshopper, framed pictures of grandpa.
She wrapped with her hands my mother's hands

around each remnant, their skin wimpled as clouds,
sifting backward, to light's soft beginning.

We Were Already Memories

"All those moments will be lost in time…"
— Roy Batty, *Blade Runner* (1982)

Joyce draped her right leg
over my father's right leg, his leg hair
stark against her vein's blue tendrils.

I lay across them, comfortable enough.
We'd played tennis. We fell into each other
to watch the dark cover the courts.
We were already memories.

I can feel now
the weight of their bodies
inside of my body

the way, I guess, my mother
must've felt me move inside of her,
a quick heel poke, the drag of my knuckles
under her belly,

then something snapped,
something always snaps us back.

To Fathers

"To honor you, Shidoshi."

— Frank Dux, *Bloodsport* (1988)

Maybe because I ended up face-down
on a couch cushion, arm right angled
behind my back; maybe because in memory
I want to think of myself thinking

of the couch cushion's stitch-work,
all those diagonals; maybe
because I couldn't see my father's eyes;
because of the way he said

throw a punch; maybe because
Van Damme no longer made things simple
(maybe we rented *Bloodsport* too many times);
maybe because he told me he was sorry,

and if he didn't, it didn't matter;
maybe I wanted it. Maybe I want it.

Reeling

"Yippi ki yay, motherfucker."
— John McClane, *Die Hard* (1989)

I remember it as a dull ringing
that scrambled my brain into pixel fuzz,

like a film that's left you reeling,
puzzling the reservoir of living

that leaches from you careful as tree moss.
I remember it as a dull ringing,

the muffled sound of demented singing,
my backyard moved to sunlessness,

a scene from a film that leaves you reeling.
I watched myself become the old haunting,

addled by scolds, slowed by Mother's caress.
I remember it as a dull ringing,

the rock I threw, the unsuspecting
squirrel felled from the fence lifeless.

Like a film that's left you reeling,
there was no climax, no clamoring,

just a dead squirrel, a boy motionless.

To Stepfathers

Philip, my mother must've said, her voice
thick like guilt, *he stole your fucking money.*
She'd swallow the *fuck* like a throat lump.
Phil must've stood there, a wet quilt draped

over a clothesline. But he always stood
like that, and she always said *fuck*ing like that,
when it mattered, when what cohered them
softened. They cornered me in the den.

I was stoned and watching *Predator.* Carl Weathers
hissed at Arnold, blood on his breath: *you're an asset,
an expendable asset.* The day before I stole
200 bucks from Phil's office safe.

I bought a bag of weed, smoked
most of it that day. *Matthew*, she said,
her voice thick like guilt, *Phil
would like to talk with you.* He stood there,

a wet quilt draped over a clothesline.
Arnold stepped into a clearing, stared
discerningly into a tree top. The "predator"
stared back in infrared scrambles, listening.

It was trying to discern language, it was
trying to understand something it couldn't.

III.

To Teachers

"ah, ah, ah, I love counting feelings."
— Count von Count, "Once More with Feelings," *Sesame Street* (2007)

All I thought I had to do was teach,
then I overheard one of my students,
before class, explain how he and Aidan
and Hunter, a few days earlier, found
a bowling ball, somewhere, and took it,
of all places, to an abandoned school,
then counted, like teenage Count von
Counts, the smacks of concrete before
the bowling ball split. When asked why,
he looked indignant. *We wanted to see*
what it was made of, he snarked.
We had to break it open to understand
what it was made of. The bell rang,
seats were taken. I closed the door, took roll.

Freshman English

"Because the longer you wait to begin, the less likely you are to find it at all."

— John Keating, *Dead Poets Society* (1989)

The girl in the back,
with thin classroom light
catching the glitter
on her eyelids, with her
slight head cocked,
extended her arm
and rotated her hand,
as if to say, *Hey, let's go,*
I've got things to do,
as if the spheres
of her adulthood visions
and the bubbly,
cursive notes in the margins
of her *Twilight* novel
intersected, like the Venn
Diagram I drew on the white board —
as if she lived in the collection
of finite sets, as if
she understood that moments
of purpose glimmer,
like glitter on eyelids,
in thin light.

Linoleum Dojo

"Go, find balance."

— Miyagi, *The Karate Kid* (1984)

In the end the karate kid unfurls
poised to flap, his lumbering neck exposed
as if survival lingered unpinioned,
as if Miyagi, empty toll of temple bells,
frog splash of evening's hushed pond,
couldn't feel Daniel's uneven toes tingle,
as if he didn't know the auditorium's
shifting dust. Unstitched from the sofa, I crane
kick to the kitchen, across Zen linoleum,
pause as branches slope over night sky
and descend upon meandering fruit flies.
The window's reflection beguiles.
Miyagi appears. He taps his heart
as if to say, *karate here, Matthew-san.*
Pots and pans whisper their quiet witchery,
the microwave's socket om's like a monk.
Miyagi's eyes are basins, the stove's two
burners, the two-bulb light — two fruit flies,
night after night, on the reflection's face,
the reflection's face.

Chinatown

"Forget it, Jake. It's Chinatown."
                    — Walsh, *Chinatown* (1974)

His mouth twitched like a frown
forming, but it didn't.
"Forget it, Jake. It's Chinatown,"

I said, thinking the line was well placed, laid down
witty enough. It wasn't.
Danny's mouth moved around

for something to say that might drown
out another one-liner I bent
toward obscurity. "Chinatown?

Really? You haven't seen it?" The crown
of his knuckles turned white. "Fuck, Matt."
His mouth parted, a hospital gown

untied. "You try to be profound
and come off stupid. I just told you some heavy shit
and you act douchey...*forget it, it's Chinatown*

(he mocked). You're an emotional fuckin' clown."
I wasn't listening, I couldn't believe he hadn't seen it.
Gaw, the last scene? Danny looked down
to his drink. *Forget it, Danny. Chinatown.*

Snickers Bar Kid

"Yeah, sure. Don't worry about it, it's no problem."
— Danny McGrath, *Billy Madison* (1993)

Not a talker, this kid, eyes like a lake's leafy floor,
so his lurch, like his stomach swallowed itself,
is overlooked, lost in lunchroom din. Under

the tables leg triangles rotate, invert, knee-nock, validate
in the naked way of teenagers a place in their lunchroom:
a boy with man-thick stubble troubled to hide his hands,

a lunchless girl jaw-clicking, her friend that spreads
herself over conversation like so much mayo.
They didn't know the kid, just the rumors —

how he slipped Visine into Mrs. Kirkpatrick's coffee,
called in the bomb threat last April, drank the blood
of rats in the boiler room — they only knew his strained
        face,

the epilepsy of recognition after he puked on shoes,
lunch trays, Pepsi cans. They'd point, they'd laugh
(a few would shit in his parent's mailbox). But the kid

carried on, slipped slightly in his puke, dabbled
his chin with a torn napkin. We'd call him
a Snickers bar kid, the kind of kid we'd give a Snickers to

if we ever had him in our offices; an effort, we'd joke,

"to keep off his list," the list we imagined he drafted,
staring out his bedroom window, into night's fetid
corners.

Mortician

"Why don't we just pretend he didn't die? Just for a bit!"
                                    — Larry, *Weekend at Bernie's* (1989)

I walked away when they said how peaceful
Danny seemed; how perfect now for God,
God who cares little for renderings:
the way the asphalt and the windshield
shifted his face; the duet of shit and piss
darkening his jeans; the allegro of wind
rustling his hair into unblinking eyes,
like thrummed weeds over roadside debris.
I've composed for weeks in the dim light
of my head's sewer, beneath the trodden
thoroughfare's memory-traffic, angling
his gurney from chromatic dust; plucking
glass from his cheeks; washing clean the blood;
rearranging cold skin; harmonizing
lips, nose, the eyes; whistling while working
something like "Amazing Grace," which is
to say, the sound of my tissue clamp,
the closest I can get to the tune.

Fifth Date

"God , I hope he doesn't turn out to be a schmuch like the others."

—— Annie, *Annie Hall* (1977)

When Esme kicked the exercise ball my way
I stared at her, as I did when she wasn't
looking, like through fading light, with only
the language of her smothered nipples,
of that diamond of air between her thighs
and crotch, to guide through darkness the pale ghosts
of my pride. Before the challenge, before
her foot rolled to me the taut ball, she planked
herself on it, did 20 reps and paused
in perfect push-up position, like some
steel joist for me to place in hoisting
us from the earth to the light of what would be,
where her eyes adjust to my position
on the ball: unsure arms, arched back,
buckling knees, crooked beams steely in hope.

Honeymoon

*"By the way, is there anyone on board who knows how to fly a
plane?"*

— Elaine Dickinson, *Airplane* (1980)

I remember those movies
where those *anyones* fly these things,
in terrorist takeovers, in cabin ruptures,
when pilots roll over dead:

Those reluctant heroes unbuckled
like their safety belts — the terse veteran,
the unassuming doctor, the sheepish stewardess,
those who fumble into courage then billow

like clouds back to their misshapen anonymity.
I scratch out aimless shapes, napkin-stretched
pen marks beneath the moist ring of my plastic glass.
The plane jumps, my *Coke* squirms.

Relax, Esme says. *Rough air . We're not gonna die.*
They don't let just anyone fly these things.

Someone Steals The Words

"People are always telling you that change is a good thing."
— Kathleen, *You've Got Mail (1998)*

As if the buildings stand for us,
as if the antsy bustle below bows
for us — an old scene in an old movie,
in love, out of love, in the park
they find it again, when the city halts
for two hands that touch for too long:
They'll be fine, they're going to make it;
they'll live as long as the lie can last.
I turn from the skyline; misplaced light
disrupts the frame. Esme's already
moved to the leaf toddling for the hill's slope.
Two kids jump through errant light pocked
on soft swing set padding. They laugh
(Esme thinks he sends us their laughter
on the wind). The leaf in Esme's hand shivers.
What was going to be isn't. We are here.
Esme traces a sun-struck vein, she holds the leaf
hard at its fingers. Somewhere the sun
is placed just right, somewhere a park bench
illuminates, someone knows what to do,
what to say; someone steals the words —
they belong to me.

To Wives

"Leave the gun. Take the cannoli."
                    — Clemenza, *The Godfather* (1972)

The cannoli buckled
and it was all Clemenza could do
to grip the soft twine
that held the box together.

Clemenza's wife busied herself
with things about the house
swollen on her doughy ankles
waiting for his return.

He paused at the front steps
tidied the white box
daubed Pauly's blood
with licked fingers.

The package sustained him
and it was all Clemenza could do
to let slip the soft twine
that held the box together.

IV.

August

"Have you ever heard of insect politics?"
>   — Seth Brundle, *The Fly* (1986)

We play a card game at the beach.
Esme's family teaches me, annoyed with
my inapprehension. The cards move fast,
too fast. Mine don't. I'm lost, panicked,
whizzing like a bug in a jar — each round's
a fit of quick card swats, eye scans, swift hands.
It's August. Outside night clouds zig-zag
to us with the surf: sand shimmies, water hisses,
a weaver spider works its web over
the beach access walk. Behind my in-laws
the TV flashes, its volume turned low,
and illuminates the table in faint strobes —
Cronenberg's *The Fly* , that scene where
Veronica consoles Seth mid-metamorphosis.
Seth jerks his head, his ear dislodges,
slides to his feet. Seth looks rueful.
Veronica muffles her gasp with shaky fingers.

Pieces

"A director makes only one movie in his life.
Then he breaks it into pieces and makes it again."

— Jean Renoir

The Birds

You must've been the final thing Phil saw,
you must've held a tune while you porpoised.
You must've swooned in cinematic awe,
you must've been the final thing he saw.
You must've scattered when the bullet lost
shape through his head, you must've moved with purpose.
You must've been the final thing Phil saw;
you must've held a tune while you porpoised.

The Kitchen Window

No one could know how you'd frame it but you,
no architect or builder or laborer:
Phil's lifelessness tucked in your domestic milieu?
No one could know how you'd frame it but you,
no "cut!" called could shift that moment — two
birds mocked Phil's silence? You petulant director,
no one could know how you'd frame it but you,
the architect, the builder — our labor.

The Grass

You absorbed the life that spilled out of him.
Still, my mother asked me to clean the blood stain

45

(I think of Frost, that hideous metonym).
You absorbed the life that spilled out of him.
Sprawled on you — she saw — she called them —
the paramedics. I never wished more for rain.
You absorbed the life that spilled out of him.
My mother asked me to clean the blood stain.

The Bullet

You saw something we could never see,
you cut through synapses like film edits.
You were gentle in your surgery?
You rearranged his stock completely,
you made mush the hard strain of his ancestry.
You found the script for pain and read it,
you saw something we could never see;
you cut through synapses like film edits.

The Cat

You followed him everywhere, you must've known,
you weaved through his legs purring, pleading:
he shut the screen door, you looked down
at your paws—you couldn't follow, you must've known—
you paced the door's width, then around
the chair to the window, paws to screen, kneading:
you followed him everywhere, you must've known,
you weaved through his legs pleading?

Ghosts

"I am but a shadowy reflection of you."
                    — Belloq, *Raiders of the Lost Ark* (1981)

Jack plucked a Wise Man from the nativity
on the end table. Two months ago
everything was a ghost, all the white shrouds
hanging from trees and doors and porches.
So when he came to me, the Wise Man
regal in his little fingers, he bellowed
Gho , Gho — his attempt at saying *ghost*,
his only framework for understanding.
And he wasn't wrong. The wicker rendition
reeks of hands that held it before him.
He holds it like a prize, like Indy did
in *Raiders of the Lost Ark*, when he grabbed
the golden idol that illuminated his face,
just before the temple crumbled.

Year Seven

"Ditto."

— Sam Wheat, *Ghost* (1990)

Now, time is carved out for touching —
as if that mushy pottery scene in *Ghost*
went like this: Demi Moore takes
her foot off the pedal, Swayze stands

awkwardly, his fingers reach for his palms,
his inner wrists twitch. She takes them,
like discipline, around her waist as he sits,
she puts his hands on the clay. He's thinking

about the shower he didn't take,
the second day sweaty in his jeans.
She thinks about sleep, which she didn't think
a second ago. She fingers the clay,

he feels her fingers finger the clay.
When it's over, they clean the mess in silence.

If Anything

"Never recreate from your memory. Always imagine new places."

— Cobb, *Inception* (2010)

Phil had a Nordic Track in the basement
and I'd glare at him as I shut the door
hoping to watch TV without hearing his breath.

Funny what we aren't. In those moments
and this one he jiggles, chest hair curled
and pasted by sweat. I was hoping, here,

now, for the opiate of memory,
for imagination's sweet sanctifier.
But he swishes the tethered handles,
slaps the wooden skis on the tracks, jiggles.

He'd finish his work out. He'd open the door,
pasty, lumbering, a head band pushed
too high on his head. If anything, I forget
ordinary beauty. If anything I forget grace.

To Strangers

"Why'd you call me?"

— Chiron, *Moonlight* (2016)

My buddy calls, his turn
in our once-in-a-blue-moon-ness,
in our need to tell ourselves
that we're not strangers.
We catch up with terrible quips
we've heard, snippets of pain
from those we say we love: Scott's
back in rehab, Jimmy hit a road biker
on the way back from the bar,
Anthony's divorce. We strain conversation
for as long as we pretend our interest allows,
then the beautiful chaos of home:
my four-year-old's tears, dishes clanking,
his five-year-old's tears —
I'm on the damn phone! —
the whirr of wind he makes
moving to a different room,
as if quiet was ever actually
necessary for us.
Yo, did you see Moonlight? *He asks.*
Naw, I didn't, you know how it goes, busy.
Yeah. You should see it.
It's really fuckin good.

What We Cannot Give

"This house has many hearts."
　　　　　　　— Tangina, *Poltergeist* (1982)

I wake to Rose, horror-movie-silent,
prodding my arm then ribs then cheek.
She wants in our bed, hers is too
"crweepy, daddy." When I say no,
she's possessed, on fire with the rage
that's in me too. And now I'm up,
kneeling by the edge of the bed,
hands on her knees to unhinge the swing
of her legs. Jack starts to wail, and Esme,
rubbing her forehead, her tank top
rippled over her right breast, is tender,
but fails to console her. Rose sniffles
then chokes on her tear-caked heaves,
her love like ours, mucousy, irrational,
asking for what we cannot give.

Fade Out

"Now. You're looking at now, sir. Everything that happens now, is happening now."
                    — Colonel Sandurz, *Spaceballs* (1987)

Imagine my reflection
in the TV screen's black, after the film,
after I crawled like an infection
to turn the TV off. In it,
I saw you, me, projections,
I saw how I won't get this right —
or Rose's birth, or the way the birds
scattered for Phil, or Esme reading this,
or Jack, someday, reading this, or you.
In it, Phil introduced me as his son —
my father, miles away, could hear him?
(My mother put these pages down,
saw the light dance across her windows.)
In it, I can hold different truths
the way Jack fits in my hands.
In it, I won't get this right,
and the story will be true.

About the Author

Matt LaFreniere is a husband, father, teacher, poet—not always in that order. He lives in Baltimore and teaches English at the Boys' Latin School of Maryland. You can find his most recent poems in Dunes Review, Main Street Rag, and Rat's Ass Review (other poems in Pilgrimage Magazine, Schuylkill Valley Journal, Spry, and others).

About the Press

Unsolicited Press is a small publisher in Portland, Oregon. The team aims to produce stunning books of poetry, fiction, and creative nonfiction. You can find out more at www.unsolicitedpress.com.

Lightning Source UK Ltd.
Milton Keynes UK
UKHW02f1815230718
326165UK00008B/294/P

9 781947 021396